www.BeirBuaPress.com

Selected Poems of Ned Kelly

by

Nathanael O'Reilly

Published by Beir Bua Press, March 2023

For my Irish-Australian ancestors and relatives

ISBN: 978-1-914972-59-1

Beir Bua Press, Co. Tipperary, Ireland.

Typesetting / Layout, Cover Design: Michelle Moloney King

Cover image: a visual poem by Michelle Moloney King

Ordering Information: For details, see www.BeirBuaPress.com

Published by Beir Bua Press - Printed in the UK

Our printer is certified as a B Corporation to measure our impact on the environment and help drive us to be even more conscious of our footprint.

9 781914 972591

Introduction

The poems in this collection were composed using only the words that appear in the following texts attributed to the legendary/notorious/infamous Irish-Australian bushranger Ned Kelly (1854-1880): The Jerilderie Letter, The Cameron Letter, The Babington Letter and The O'Loghlen Letter. The poems use Kelly's spelling and mimic his punctuation and capitalization. This collection was partly inspired by Peter Carey's novel *True History of the Kelly Gang* and Ian Jones's biography, *Ned Kelly: A Short Life*, along with my own visits to many of the important places in Kelly's short life (and settings for the poems). The collection attempts to answer a simple question: what if Ned Kelly wrote poetry?

Widow's Son

I am a widow's son. Is my mother
And her infant baby and my poor little
Brothers and sisters not to be pitied?
She is well acquainted with Fitzpatrick

Who took a revolver and threatened to shoot
My mother in her own house, said he would
Blow her brains out if she interfered.
She told the trooper he had no business

On her premises and it was a good job
For him Ned was not there for he would ram
The revolver down his throat & my orders
Must be obeyed. It is only foolhardiness

To disobey an outlaw. This is well known
In Greta and yet the ungrateful articles
Convicted my mother and an infant
With their cruelty and disgraceful

And cowardly conduct I being then over
400 miles from Greta and my mother's
House. I take the opportunity and give
Fair warning to all those who has reason

To fear me, and the enemy I cannot
Catch myself I shall give a payable
Reward for and them theirs and all belonging
To them exterminated off the face

Of the earth. I will not take innocent
Life if justice is given. Our country
Is woven with police and horrible
Disasters shall immediately follow.

We Irish

Our mothers and fathers and brothers
Left the ash corner deserted the shamrock
The emblem of wit and beauty
Never to see old Erins isle once more

The Queen of England was guilty she destroyed
Massacred and murdered their forefathers
Pulling their toe and finger nails rolling them downhill
In spiked barrels they were persecuted massacred

Thrown into martyrdom and tortured beyond
The ideas of the present generation more was transported
To Van Diemand's Land were doomed to Port Macquarie
Toweringabbie and Norfolk Island and Emu Plains

Those places of tyranny and condemnation
And every torture imaginable or fled to America
Or other countries to bloom again another day
But there never was such a thing as Justice

In the English laws my own brothers
What would England do if America declared war
And hoisted a green flag as its all Irishmen
That has got command of her armies forts and batteries

Even her very life guards and beef tasters are Irish.
Many a blooming Irishman rather than subdue
To the Saxon yoke were flogged to death and bravely died
In servile chains murdered on their own soil

Horses and Cattle

On the 29th of March I was released
From prison. I was never convicted
Of horse stealing therefore I started wholesale
And retail horse and cattle dealing.

When the horses were found on the Murray
I sold them afterwards at Benalla
And the rest in New South Wales
And left Victoria as I wished

To see certain parts of the country.
The horses were sold as straight
As the Germans over the Murray
Would swear to anyone

All the stray horses and the culls were kept
In Petersons paddock. Two was sold
To Kennedy and the rest to Baumgarten
Taking their horses and their brands altered by me

William Cooke who was convicted for Whitty's horses
Was innocent he was not in my company
At Petersons. And my step-father George King
Stealing Whitty's horses and selling them

The pick of them was sold at Howlong
He was doing a good trade at Oxley
With the stealing and selling of the horses
To acquaint the Auctioneer and to advertise

My horses for sale as I have sold horses
And cattle innumerable and yet eight head
Of the culls is all ever was found
Out of over thirty head of the very best horses

The pick of them was taken to a good market
And I sold some of them in Benalla
And Melbourne and other places I was told
I was blamed for stealing this bull

From Whitty & his son-in-law Farrell very remarkable
Branded (M) Flood used to claim the brand
Was altered I asked Whitty at Oxley racecourse
Why he blamed me for stealing his bull

When he killed him for beef their hounds were barking
At the wrong stump. He is the greatest horsestealer
With the exception of myself and George King
I know of. Farrell the Policeman stole a horse

From George King & told Whitty he heard I sold
The bull to Carr. I was blamed for stealing a mob
Of calves I was accused of stealing Whitty's horses
But Constable Flood stole and sold most of them

I have known over 60 head of horses impounded
In one day for no man could steal their horses & cattle
Without the knowledge of the poor.
Not long afterwards I heard again I was blamed

For stealing a mob of calves from Whitty
And Farrell which I knew nothing about.
Mr. Johns had a horse called Ruita Cruta
And had him in Whitty and Farrell's paddocks

Until Mr. Brown of the Laceby Station got him shifted
He sold him to Carr a Publican and Butcher
He had some conversation with a horse dealer
And George King. One bay cob he stole and sold

Four different times I was arrested on the charge
Of horsestealing which any man can see is false
And on Hall and Murdoch's evidence prove a conviction
Of horse-stealing against me. Any man knows

It is possible to swear a lie. Whitty and Burns
Not being satisfied brought more charges
Against me Accused me of stealing a mare I was Innocent
Of knowing the mare to be stolen. Girls used to ride her about

I was acquitted of stealing but I was found guilty of receiving
Convicted on the evidence of the meanest man ever the sun
Shone on as the stock society offered an enticement
I can say I never was convicted of horse or cattle stealing

Constable Hall

Hall was a lazy loafing cowardly
Great cur more like the species of a baboon
Or Gorilla than a man. Big & ugly
Enough to lift Mount Macedon out

Of a crab hole. He cannot look behind
Him without turning his whole frame
For he has a head like a turnip. I heard
He sold his sister to a Chinaman.

In the first place Hall is a rogue in his heart
And was considerably in debt
To Mr. L. O'Brien. Hall has been tried
Several times for perjury but got clear

Hall's character is well known about
Eldorado and Snowy Creek
I was once arrested by Constable
Hall and 14 more men in Greta

For shooting Trooper Fitzpatrick. Hall could
Not pot me for horse stealing. Constable
Hall came to me as I was getting off my horse
Caught hold of me and thought to throw me

But made a mistake so I duped and jumped
At him & accepted the challenge.
I used to trip him and let him take a mouthful
Of dust now and again. I dare not strike him

Or my sureties would lose the bond money.
Hall never told me he wanted to arrest me
I kept throwing him in the dust. I never
Was interfered with whilst I kept up

This successful trade. I got him across the street
Where there was some brush fencing and on this
I threw big Cowardly Hall instead of putting my foot
On his neck and taking his revolver

I straddled him on his belly and rooted
Both spurs onto his thighs he roared like a calf
Attacked by dogs and shifted several yards
Of fence for I need no lead or powder to fight.

Hall was frightened and I knew he would pull the trigger
He called for assistance to a man
Named Cohen and Barnett, Lewis, Thompson,
Jewitt two blacksmiths who was looking on

Hall got up and snapped three or four caps at me
He jumped forward he tried to shoot me
A man that is such a bad shot as to miss
A man three times at a yard and a half

Beat me over the head with his six chambered
Colts revolver and caught me by the privates
I was taken by Hall and his 14
Assistants who would have sent me to Kingdom Come

It would suit them far better. I dare not strike
Any of them they would shoot me first
I was bound to keep the peace for 12 months
Or I could have spread those curs like dung

In a paddock without some civilians assistance
And when Wild Wright and my mother
Came they could trace us across the street by the blood
In the dust which spoiled the lustre

Of the paint on the gate-post of the Barracks.
Hall sent for more Police and nine stitches
Were put in some of the cuts by Dr Hastings.
The Doctor died He would have proved Hall a perjurer.

Eleven Mile Creek

I write these lines hoping to find you in good
Health as I am myself at present. I have
Arrived safe and I would like you would see what you could
Do for me. I have done all circumstances

Would allow me. Now try what you can do answer
His letter as soon as possible direct
Your letter to Daniel Kelly Gretta
Post office that is my name no more at present

Everyone looks on me like a black snake send
Me an answer as soon as possible
Or even begging his tucker I wish to acquaint
You with him and we could stand a chance released

From that land of bondage and tyranny shaking
With fear and yet there are civilians who take
Firearms against me. I will oppose your laws. I heard
I was outlawed for what reason I do not know

There is no fear of anyone stealing their property
With the rest we approached and they came
To Victoria the property of a Telegraph
Master in Mansfield he told Dan to clear out

Which will open the eyes with no offence I began
To think tar-and-feather him I did not see her
(Remember your railroads) and with the aid of this money
And a sweet goodbye from Edward Kelly

As close as we could get to the camp and inhabitants
Enforced outlaw if any man was mean enough to steal
Their property the one hit knocked the two men down but he
Would be a king to a policeman Strachan had been

Over the Murray no one interfering who billet
In good health with them as the intervening space
Being clear ground however ridiculous the evidence
May seem to give to her and came home trying

To get up a case against him and those innocent men
And a hundred pound for any man that could
Convict him and no battery and no doubt they will
Acknowledge caught the revolver with one hand

He lost her on the 6th and if I had robbed and plundered
Ravished and murdered everything I met young
And old rich and poor but no taking a hawker but follow
Me and my brother into the wilds but went back

Again for fear and make as little enemies as he can
Some of the occurrences of the present past
And future horse out of a bog Wild Wright came
To the Eleven Mile to pull Hall by the collar

With the other when she would come with all the picked
Land on the Boggy Creek and King River
I received three months or £10 as the public could
Not do any more than take firearms

Where he had been quietly digging as he shall find
If the poor is on his side he shall loose nothing by it.
With their two revolvers and fowling-piece the Police
Might come to our camp to serve under a flag

And nation and they would convict him if they caught him
While we were all away to see Mr. Gunn
Neither molesting or interfering with anyone
In or about gazetted her on the 12th of March

If they depend on the police they shall be drove
To destruction paid heavy rent for all
The open ground and cannot be no worse assisting
The police as they have done, they got up

And one took a double barrelled fowling piece
Which I loaded with bullets instead of shot.
He was making good wages dropped his revolver
And ran. Manure Bullock Flat with us on our arrival.

Stopped all night instead of giving and I was a prisoner
And the run of their stock on certificate
Ground free as Baumgarten and Kennedy Williamson
And Skillion and got 3 years experience

In Beechworth and Pentridge's dungeons as the creek
Is very rich within half a mile from where
I shot Kennedy. As they can not and will not
Protect them but by the light that shines I stopped

At the logs knew I wish to state a fair chance to try
Your pluck I have been told by police that he
Is hardly ever sober by the greatest of torture
Pegged on an ant-bed with their bellies opened

He could not live, or I would have let him go
And fetched a horse down I fired again
With the gun for hitting him and have but once to die
And Dan went back to the spring of 1870

Of what they were convicted for if I gave myself up
To her duffing and bushranging were abolished
The police would have to cadge for their living
And no one interfering with them for witnesses

To swear anything I was not there long and lost his mare.
This is the only charge ever proved against me
Outcasts and outlaws all the picked land on King River
And Boggy Creek. In Beechworth Gaol until the 29th

Paid heavy rent to the banks for fear the troopers
Would come one drove the horses down I speak
From experience for all the open ground and on
The 25th of October I enquired

After my brother Dan I wrote a letter to Mr
Swanhill of Lake Rowan and revolver and he
Did not expect them that night and the Germans over
The Murray would swear to the wrong man

Between Table Top and the bogs. and he found neither
Of us were dead got up in the morning to feed
His horses those being on sentry looked all day for her
Will be fool as well as the right and found him

Digging on Bullock Creek. My Brother Dan was never
Charged with assaulting a woman I crossed them
And returning in the evening and so as a poor man
Could keep no stock, the ground was very soft

Therefore I could not have stole the mare as he was helpless
As a big goanna after leaving a dead bullock
Or horse I brought some of them to that place and could
Not with some of them but he was sentenced

To 3 months without the option of a fine he would summons
Me to pine their young lives away in starvation
And misery and impounded every beast they could get
But did not sell I told him no or I would have let him

Go he reached for his revolver and jumped off
They sold his sister to a Chinaman
I came on a different lot of tracks and a poor man
Could not keep his stock whatever I would shoot

No man and one month and two pound fine even off
Government roads and knew he had strayed
Used to be blowing among tyrants worse than the promised
Hell itself on the off side of his horse

For damaging property and if he gave up his arms
And leave the force making for the shingle hut
A poor man happened to leave his horse they would not ask
Me to stand got behind a tree which they would have done

Had their bullets been directed as they intended them.
Brutally treating any of them, it is a cruel
Falsehood or bit of a poddy calf outside his paddock
A sentence that there is no law to uphold

About two miles and take notice of it and told my brother
And his two mates and the Police got great credit
And praise therefore that was not the very spot where
Mrs. O'Brien's Hotel stands therefore

The Minister of Justice neglected his duty
In that case they would be impounded between
Greta attempting to murder him sent his man with him
And the Police searched the place and watched the papers

And then cry surrender on the Eleven Mile Creek
Their property either consumed or confiscated
Get her Wright who was a stranger as he had bad health
To gallop away but the horse would not go

And said he wanted me to sign some papers now
The cellar was just dug then I am now placed
In very peculiar circumstances to state
The facts of the case we are not so bad

As we are supposed to be. for arresting the mother
Of 12 children and how they used to rush
At the shingle hut Wright and Gunn were potted any amount
Of injustice to be had by Whitty and Burns

All belonging to poor farmers and as for Dan
Dismounting about a mile from my brother's
House, which he took to be Constable Flood and his life
Was insured, and quick as thought fired at me

And when they could not snare me was in a hurry
To get back James Murdock, who has been
Recently hung in Wagga Wagga they would have
To leave their ploughing or harvest or other

Employment to go to Oxley one an infant
On her breast upset all the milk dishes
Break tins of eggs with the rifle without unslinging it
Saw they carried long firearms and had he not

Obeyed my orders, he told me he intended going home
To Mansfield and I gave him When they would get there
And was in the act of firing again who put that article
As well as I could or attempted to reach for the gun

The land could produce. I did not sign at Beechworth
He never was tried for assaulting and those
Two quiet hard working innocent men on the ground
And were they my own brothers I could not

Have been more sorry for them writing a few lines
We will not leave it taken for aiding
And abetting if we could not beat those before
The others would come or draw his revolver

He would have been shot dead, perhaps not have money
Enough to arrest him, it was only a telegram
From Chiltern. I could only find one when I got my liberty.
Who would not know the difference a revolver

And a saucepan handle and even the meat out of the cask
He was stopping at my Mother's awaiting
Finer or dryer weather another mare and he told me
Now you are warned. Who had no protection

But when I called on them and also about the Police
As I knew the other party to release them
Whom he swore was William Skillion what would people say
If I became a policeman concerning

My bail bonds and kept them six months awaiting trial
And destroy all the provisions or lie down
And let them shoot me They are worse than cold-blooded
Murderers & hangmen. This man was not called

And have to give a bill of sale would soon join them to throw
Up their hands I warn you that within a week
We will leave your Colony I was about 14
Years of age Dan said "Produce your Warrant"

In their ignorance and blindness it would not be wilful
Murder and took an oath to arrest my brothers
And sisters & relations he knows as much about Commanding
Police as Standish does about mustering

Mosquitoes concerning the case and shove the girls
He told me the NSW Police had shot
A man for shooting Sergeant Walling and then convicted
And if they came on us at our camp besides

Several other Witnesses to the navvies on the railway
Line or borrow the money which is no easy
Matter in front of them to the rising generation
On the evidence of the meanest article

That ever the sun shone on and boiling them down
For their fat they would shoot us down like dogs
I told him if they did they had shot the wrong man
Mr. Butler, P.M. and convict them

By fair or foul means until he brought mine back
Sentenced him to 3 months without the option
Of a fine. Had I robbed, plundered, ravished and murdered
Everything I met. I was going to Wangaratta and along

With all this sort of work we had only two guns
And I expect your gang came to do the same with me
They would have got great praise as well as promotion
Into the rooms like dogs and one month or 2 pounds fine

For wilfully destroying property. the mosquitoes
Were very bad he had just got to the logs
On the back blocks of the Lachlan a sentence
Which there is no law to uphold it seems

The jury was well chosen by the Police and yet
They had to do their sentence after the conviction
Of my Mother the line was completed and the men gone
And their prosecutor which they generally are

I am reckoned a horrid brute and gave them if not
Mr. D. Goodman since got 4 years
For perjury when I came out and Flood was shifted
To Oxley so as if anyone was there

And put his head up to take aim he said the papers
Was at the Barracks I got his hands at the back
Of his neck. After leaving this man he went to the house
And the persecutions and insults offered

Until he left the force as there was a discharged Sergeant
Amongst them and bail those up take their firearms
Concerning the same property and my fist came
In collision with McCormick's nose and seen the mare

I caught back them up to their utmost then I shot him
That instant which is contrary to law
Because I had not been cowardly enough to lie down
For them he carried on the same game there

He asked was Dan in I told Gould that was for his good
Nature and ammunition and horses
They thought it impossible for a Policeman to swear
A lie and all this was the cause of me

The trooper looked around to see if it was true.
A stiff neck as big as his shoulders
They used to repeatedly rush into the house
Revolver in hand and upset milk dishes

Empty the flour out onto the ground break tins of eggs
Throw the mat out of the cask onto the floor
And dirty and destroy all the provisions Dan came out
Under such trying circumstances laid the gun

Against a stump and yet a policeman is still worse
And guilty of meaner actions and tried
To make him let the revolver go or he would have shot me
But I can assure them it is by that means

But they knew well I was not there thank God
And insults to my people narrow hipped and pointed
Towards the feet like a vine stake and took her with me
During my stay on Moyhu Racecourse

They would have to leave their harvest or ploughing
I run in a wild bull although a gelding I would
Have scattered their blood and brains like rain any time
Without an owner as I took him to be Strachan

And hiring cads they get promoted and caused him to lose
His equilibrium and fall prostrate
All the Police and Detective. The Queen must surely
Be proud of such heroic men as the Police

And Irish soldiers certainly their wives and children
Are to be pitied. He had no murderous
Intention but he stuck to it like grim death to a dead
Volunteer and selling them to Baumgarten

Mrs. Kelly asked him what he wanted Dan for
I have heard from a trooper three dozen
For the fowling piece Mrs. McCormick turned on me
The minister of justice no easy matter

And I had no idea he wanted to arrest me
Not in the Police Gazette he asked Dan
To come to Greta with him the man who said he would
Not ask me to stand he would shoot me first

Like a dog I am myself at present escaped
From Wangaratta. They used to come to the house
When there was no one there but women
We had nothing but a gun and a rifle

I tied up my horse to finish the battle as I hear
He gets as much pay as a dozen good troopers
If there is any good in them as it takes eight
Or eleven of the biggest mud crushers

In Melbourne to take one poor little half starved larrikin
To a watch house. He was as clever as old Wombat
He never knew Fitzpatrick but it happened to be Lonigan
A picked jury the man who in company

With Sergeant Whelan Fitzpatrick and King the Bootmaker
And constable O'Day that tried to put a pair
Of hand-cuffs on me in Benalla but could not and God
Knows how many they were and what does he do

I have seen as many as eleven, and yet they know
And acknowledge I have been wronged
If she interfered in the arrest or any other
Stallion but McCormick got up and ran

He blamed me Berrill seen her as Martins had away
With the rifle this looked to be one night sober
Dan said all right and had to allow McInnis the miller
To put them on instead of going to the Barracks.

He was always running his horses about. They got ropes
Tied my hands and feet. That is my name no more
At present see all the men I have out today as if
They meant not only to shoot me

They both went inside the Police camp I gave him my word
I would give them a chance amongst which was a retired
Sergeant of Police running horses away but not wishing
To take their lives we waited neither molesting

Or interfering with any poor men of the district.
He looks a young strapping rather genteel
Only to riddle me we had no chance, only to die
Like dogs should enquire into this respecting

Their sentence He said he was sure they would never follow
I will have as many more tomorrow. Constable Hall
Asked me what the row was about town during several days
Gould knew that he was wicked, could not catch himself

I don't know either Kennedy Scanlon or him
And had nothing against them, I was fined
Two pounds for hitting Fitzpatrick he will find a wrong
Jurisdiction for fear of body snatchers.

From Greta swamp to the Seven Mile Creek I told him
They accused also who has no alternative
Stopped at Peter Martin's Star Hotel in Wangaratta
For a keen observer the trial of my mother

He said he would get them to give up arms and two pounds
For not allowing and taking them on his beat
And them armed with battens and neddies do something
Towards the release of those innocent men I have known

Over sixty head of horses to be in one day
Impounded into the wilds where he had been
Quietly digging consequently he enticed McCormick's
Horse away from Greta but Flood can make a cheque

Single-handed. They were strangers to me and I believe
Honest men. The trooper said he had a warrant
For him, he has the wrong appearance only to put up
With the brutal and cowardly conduct

If I would not shoot them as small as paper
That is in our guns they paid me full
Value for the horses she was a chestnut as quick
As thought fired at me with the rifle

David Lindsay who gave evidence for the crown
Or a manly heart if so why not send
The men that gets big pay and reckoned superior
To the common police after me

McCormick accused me of using their horse mare
White face docked tail on October 19
1877 at Benalla. Mr. Gould was up early
And I hit McCormick. I worked on a farm

Some of them going to the hospital could not have known
They were stolen. Dan then asked him to produce
The warrant. The deceit and cowardice is too plain
As I could not blame them, said he would blow her

Brains out feeding his horses and I would do the same
To him and you shall soon save the country
Of high salaries six months awaiting trial and no bail
Allowed from the effects of hits from the fists

Of the Larrikin a horse and saddle was never traced
After leaving employment Detective Ward
And Constable Hayes took out their revolvers
Only I was not ready. No person had anything to do

As plain as the hands on a town clock
Next morning I was handcuffed to be seen
In the puny cabbage hearted looking face and he
Is the man that blowed before he left Violet Town

For shooting at a trooper in Victoria and destroying
Their provisions. Beside shooting a trooper to men
That is fit for nothing but getting better men shot.
They did not know me a perfect Stranger

And my Uncle was cutting and branding calves
And these are the only charges was ever proved
Against either of us. If he challenged me
They had to do their duty heard a bell

And the Magistrate would send the poor
Little larrikin into a dungeon. Since February 1873
I worked as a faller at Mr. J. Saunders
And R Rules sawmills. He said it was a telegram

A shanty keeper having no licence I heard
Nothing of this transaction if Ned Kelly
Was to be shot he was the man would shoot him
Who some calls honest gentlemen

For being a better man than such a parcel
Of armed curs. I came on the track of police
Horses between Table Top and the Bogs
Sent from Chiltern then for Heach and Dockendorff

A rope tied from them to my legs and to the seat
Of the cart I said I did not blame them
For doing honest duty and came on the broad of his back
Himself until very close on the trial

For the Detectives and other evil disposed persons
No doubt would shoot me even if I threw up my arms
And laid down my revolver. Until he left the force
Sergeant Whelan ordered him to relieve Steel at Greta

Taken to Wangaratta I never worked
For less than two pound ten a week.
He knew four of them could not arrest me
As short a time as possible after reading

This notice for he knew the horse well.
In Mrs. Skillion's absence seen McCormick's
Horses and keeps a book of information
For the police. He sent his boy to take him back

To Emu Swamp wrote a note and gave it to me
Went to Greta to call and arrest Dan
And take him into Wangaratta single-handed
Not to talk of the rest of my mates

Since I left Pentridge we are falsely represented
As it makes no difference to them
They get their living by lying, either me or him
Would have to die in my own native land.

In 1875 or 1876 I was overseer
For Saunders and Rule. Get him remanded
No matter how deprived would not be guilty
He pulled out his revolver. A man that knows nothing

About roguery would never enter the force. Hundreds
Of charges of horsestealing was against me.
His character needs no comment. They came straight out
To Gould and accused Dan of working the horse.

We could have shot those two men without speaking
And swore their lies against me had the right parties
Been convicted. Such a cowardly action so he tied me
Whilst Constable Arthur laughed at his cowardice

But it will give Them a chance of showing
Whether they are worth more pay
Than a common trooper or not.
And they knew Fitzpatrick wronged us

Which shall be worse than the rust in the wheat
In Victoria. Dan's mother said Dan need not go
Without a warrant this he knew well
Therefore he had a right to keep out of my road

This was false besides other important evidence
Which can be brought on the prisoner's behalf
It would have been a bad job for the Police unless
He liked a strapping and genteel young man

Gould was amazed at the idea. I was sentenced
For it was he who escorted me and Hall
To Wangaratta. I will show you we are determined
Men. He is capable of rendering

Fitzpatrick any assistance he required
For a conviction. McCormick said
He would fight me. Would they not slew around
And fight her with their own arms if required

And to have a case and conviction if possible
And putting him in the lock up I could not
Help laughing as Mrs. Kelly said that if Ned
Was here to hear three months

As he could be broke any time. I was tried
And committed. Since I was on the King
River this shows my feeling towards him
Without some Authority besides his own word

To my brothers and sisters who had no protection
And obtaining money under false pretences,
I believe, an honest man for the sake of the colour
They dare not wear they both went inside

Only I came to their aid coupled with the conviction
Of my mother. As he said we were good friends
And even swore it we came to the conclusion
I was then fourteen years of age

For hitting him during my stay there I tried
To catch the mare Hall swore I claimed
And those men certainly made my blood boil
To a keen observer he has the wrong appearance

To have anything like a clear conscience
Or a manly heart as to send his boy
For years and to reinstate it and rise.
And if a policeman loses a conviction

For the sake of swearing a lie he has broke his oath
Therefore he is a perjurer either ways.
And three months for the parcel I am really astonished
To see the mare Trying to get up a case

They impounded every beast they could catch
I ran in a wild bull as I don't think there is a man born
And good employment and got them double pay
The intervening space being clear

He had the presence of mind to know his position
To take him from the Ruta Cruta and take him back
To them. If they were my own brothers
I could not be more sorry for them

And the coroner should be consulted
And bound to keep the peace
I gave to Lydecker a farmer the deceit
Directly as he was spoken to

The pressure and tyrannism of the English yoke
Searched the Eleven Mile Creek
And every other place in the district for me.
The trooper left and invented some scheme

To say he got shot in the arrest. The police
Could not have the patience to suffer
It as long as I did and he can be thankful
I was not there. I was getting off my horse

Stringybark Creek

I have no intention of asking mercy for myself
Or any mortal man or apologising
To Members of the Legislative Assembly led astray
Or to ever allow his blood to get cold

The trooper was impatient not alone
To the mother that suckled his white
Cabbage-hearted-looking face.
My brother-in-law and another man

Who was innocent would ram the revolver
Down his throat and he would
Still annoy my brothers and sisters. Our doom
Was sealed unless we could take their fire-arms

They would have shot me but the colts
Patent refused. I came into Victoria
And enquired after my brother
And found him working with a man

In Bullock Creek who killed cattle for beef.
Dan looked out and said Ned is coming now.
It was cowardice that made Lonigan
And the others fight and the ignorant unicorns

Even threaten to shoot myself in every paper
that is printed as this is no crime in the Police force
I am called the blackest and coldest
blooded murderer ever on record

If you knew how I have been wronged and persecuted
you would say I cannot be blamed
I was outlawed without cause. Circumstances
Have forced us to become what we are

I don't think I would use a revolver
to shoot a man like James Whitty.
If my people do not get justice
There will be no more police

I came on Police tracks I told my mates
And me and my brother went out next morning
And found police camped at the Shingle Hut
With long fire-arms. I came on more police tracks

Making for our camp. Me and my brother
Went and found their camp. We saw two men
At the logs we could have shot these two men
Without speaking, but not wishing to take life

We waited we thought there were more men
in the tent asleep. The trooper being off
His guard looked out we might have a chance
Of fighting them if we had fire-arms

As it generally takes forty to one
I have never interfered with any person
Unless they deserved it
What else can England expect

They were all Catholics before the Saxons
and Cranmore yoke held sway
And caused them to wear the enemy's coats.
What would people say if they saw

A strapping big lump of an Irishman
Paid to torment and drive me
One took a double-barrel fowling piece
Too cowardly to follow it up

Without having the force to disguise it
When I was within a yard and a half of him
Until Skillion and Ryan came with horses
from Boggy Creek sometime afterwards

I would never attempt to fire into a house
Full of women and children and those innocents
Released from prison. If I get justice
I Will cry a go my Mother

I approached the camp & called on them to throw up
Their arms McIntyre obeyed I advanced
And took possession My brother advanced from the spring
Dan keeping McIntyre covered

Lonigan sat on the log we took possession
Of their revolvers and fowling piece
I asked McIntyre where his mates was he said
They had gone down the creek and that Kennedy

And Scanlon were out looking for our camp
he asked me was I going to shoot him and his mates
I told McIntyre I did not want to shoot him
Or any man that would surrender

He said he knew Fitzpatrick had wronged us
McIntyre obeyed and never attempted
To reach for his gun. McIntyre said the police
All knew Fitzpatrick had wronged us

I asked McIntyre who was in the tent he replied
No one I asked him why they carried Spencer
Rifles and breech-loading fowling pieces
And so much ammunition

For the Police was only supposed to carry
One revolver and 6 cartridges
In the revolver but they had eighteen rounds
Of revolver cartridges each and twenty-one

Spencer-rifle cartridges he said no they did not
Come to shoot me They came to apprehend me
I could have shot them without speaking
But their lives was no good to me.

I soon heard them coming up the creek
I told McIntyre to tell them to give up
Their arms He spoke to Kennedy
Who was some distance in front of Scanlon

Kennedy alighted on the off side of his horse
And got behind a tree and opened hot
Fire and Scanlon who carried the rifle slewed
His horse around to gallop away

When I had to shoot him and he fell from his horse.
Our two mates came over when they heard
The shot fired As soon as I shot Scanlon Lonigan
Jumped up and ran some six or seven yards

To a battery of logs instead of dropping
Behind the one he was sitting on
And staggered some distance from the logs
And was in the act of firing again

When I shot him. McIntyre jumped on Kennedy's
Horse and galloped away and I allowed
Him to go as I did not like to shoot him after
He surrendered. I do not call McIntyre a coward

I reckon he is as game a man as wears the jacket
My brother Dan advanced and Kennedy
Fired at him and ran Kennedy kept firing
From behind the tree he got behind

Another tree and fired at me again I followed
Him he stopped behind another tree
And fired again I shot him in the armpit
As he slewed around to surrender

I fired with the gun again and shot him
Through the right chest I did not know
That he had dropped his revolver and was turning
To surrender with his hands raised

And then fell. He dropped his revolver he surrendered
But too late I did not know he had dropped
His revolver and the bullet passed through the right side
Of his chest & he could not live

We did not kill the policemen in cold blood
We only fired on them to save ourselves
We are not cold-blooded murderers I could not
Suffer them blowing me to pieces

And let them shoot me and my innocent brother
I called on them to throw up their hands
Certainly their wives and children are to be pitied
Had they been my own brothers

I could not help shooting them or else lie down
And let them shoot me. Those men came
Into the bush with the intention of shooting me
Down like a dog. Those men came into the bush

With the intention of scattering pieces
Of me and my brother all over
The bush to pack our remains in shattered
Into a mass of animated gore

Yet they know and acknowledge I have been wronged
This cannot be called wilful murder
I was compelled to shoot them, I was compelled
To shoot them in my own defence

Or lie down like a cur and die. The reports
Of bullets being fired into the bodies
Of the Troopers after death is false.
And as for handcuffing Kennedy

To a tree or cutting his ear off or brutally
Treating any of them is a falsehood
If Kennedys ear was cut off
It was not done by me. I put his cloak over him

And left him I put his cloak over him and left him
As honourable as I could
And if there is any one to be called a murderer
Regarding Kennedy, Scanlon and Lonigan

It is that misplaced poodle Superintendent Smith.
It will pay Government to give those people
Who are suffering innocence justice
And liberty. If the public do not see justice done

The poor would rise out to a man and find them
If they were on the face of the earth.
I wish those men who joined the stock Protection
Society to withdraw their money and give it

And as much more to the widows and orphans
And to subscribe a sum and give it to the poor
Of their district. Neglect this and abide
By the consequences it will always pay

A rich man to be liberal with the poor to sell out
And give £10 out of every hundred towards
The widow and orphan fund but they must Remember
And it is only foolishness to disobey

Everyone looks on me like a black snake
I knew I would get no justice
But wish to give timely warning Therefore
Every man's life is in danger

Fitzpatrick

On the 15th of April Fitzpatrick
Came to the Eleven Mile Creek which can be proved
By eight or nine witnesses. He asked Dan
To go to Greta with him Dan was having something to eat

My mother asked Fitzpatrick what he wanted Dan for
Fitzpatrick said they got a warrant against
My brother Dan as he had a warrant for him for stealing
I hear previous to this Fitzpatrick

Had some conversation with Williamson on the hill.
The trooper had no business on her premises
The trooper pulled out his revolver before
He would be game to put his hand on me

And he could welt me or any of my breed
Which can be proved by 8 or 9 witnesses
I took his revolver and threw him and part of the door
Outside I had a pairs of arms and bunch of fives

On the end of them and Fitzpatrick knew the weight
Of one of them only too well. Fitzpatrick
Is the only one I hit out of the five in Benalla
And he is very subject to fainting.

The trooper left and invented some scheme swearing
He was shot. Next day Williamson and my mother
Was arrested. Fitzpatrick chose to inform
On him after him being so kind. He who alone

Could have proved Fitzpatrick's falsehood. There will be
A collision between me and him and if words
Be louder they would say he ought to be ashamed
Of himself. Fitzpatrick shall be the cause

Of greater slaughter The witness which can prove Fitzpatrick's
Falsehood can be found
By advertising and we will blow him into pieces
Fitzpatrick will be the cause of greater slaughter

To the Union Jack than Saint Patrick was to the snakes
In Ireland. He was the biggest enemy I had
In the country with the exception of Hall and Lonigan
Fitzpatrick tried to choke me Lonigan caught me

By the privates and would have killed me
But was not able I did not begrudge him
What bit of lead he got. He was the flashest meanest
man that I ever had any account against

The Police

A Policeman is a disgrace to his country
The greatest ruffians and murderers
It is a credit to a Policeman to convict
An innocent man. They will lag you, guilty or not

I would like to know what business
An honest man would have in the Police
As the police are afraid or ashamed
To wear their uniform

Berry would have sacked a great many of them
And I think the Public will soon find
They are only in the road of good men
They will be sacked and supplanted by soldiers

Is there not big fat-necked Unicorns enough
Which is better known as Officers of Justice
Or Victorian Police on low pay in the towns
Who take an oath to arrest brother sister father or mother

They actually come into a court house and swear
They could not arrest one eight stone larrikin
They have got to hire cads more fit to be a starcher
To a laundress than a Policeman.

They were not satisfied with frightening my sisters
Night and day and threatened to shoot the girls
And children. Brutal and unmanly conduct of the police
That Sergeant Steel and Detective Brown and Strachan

There would be a hundred pound reward for me
Flood is different to Sergeant Steel, Strachan, Hall
And the most of Police. Five curs like Sergeant Whelan
O'Day Fitzpatrick King and Lonigan

My mother and four or five men were lagged innocent
They were not satisfied with sending orphan children
To the industrial school to make prostitutes and cads of them
They empty the flour out of the bags and go whacks

With men to steal horses and lag innocent men
Frightening and insulting my sisters night and day
Brooke. E. Smith Superintendent of Police
Reminds me of a poodle dog half clipped in the lion fashion

It takes three or four police to keep sentry
While he sleeps in Wangaratta, do they think
He is a superior animal to the men that has to guard him.
Superintendent Smith used to say to my sisters

They would shoot the girls first. It is an old saying
It takes a rogue to catch a rogue. 'Tis double pay
And country girls. An infant were taken and thrown
Into prison and is liable to a heavy fine

There was a subscription collected for Hall
They would rather riddle poor unfortunate creoles
I shall be compelled to make an example of some
Of them before morning but they will rue the day

Fitzpatrick got among them, he got James Murdock
Who was recently hung in Wagga Wagga
To give false evidence from another man.
And they wanted me to give them something to talk about.

Lagging my mother and infant
If they cannot find no other employment
Shove the girls in front of them into the rooms
Like dogs and abuse and insult them

Disgraceful conduct to my brothers and sisters
Or attempt to fire into a house where my mother
Brothers and sisters was. The police may choose
To say or swear against me impossible to get any justice

Skillion the day after heard how the Police
Detective Ward and Constable Hayes took
Out their revolvers and threatened to shoot
The girls & children certainly made my blood boil

And if they fail the Police are quite helpless.
Your policemen are cowards. Not only
The Victorian Police. But it is not the place
Of the Police to convict guilty men

I heard that I was outlawed and £100 reward
For me in Victoria. Send the high paid and men
That received big salaries for years in a gang
By themselves after me, I Heard how the police

Use to be blowing that they would shoot me first
And then cry surrender. For a while an outlaw reigns
Their pocket swells But as soon as I am dead
They will be heels up in the muroo

And also the whole British army.
Unless they want me to turn on them
And exterminate them without medicine
Any person aiding or harbouring or assisting

The Police in any way or employing any person
Whom they know to be a detective or cad
Or those who would be so depraved
As to take blood money while God gives me strength

To pull a trigger and they will be outlawed
And declared unfit to be allowed human burial
I will not exactly show them what cold-blooded
Murder is but wholesale and retail slaughter

Until we have made the country ring
With the name of Kelly and taken terrible revenge
For the injustice and oppression. And yet Remember
There is not one drop of murderous blood in my veins

As it only aids the police to procure false
Witnesses that never failed to peg out
Anything they came in contact with
To make up for this double pay and expense

McCormicks

The hawkers McCormick and his wife was camped
In Greta McCormick being a Policeman
Over the convicts in that place called Tasmania
Better known as the Dervon or Vandiemans land

He is a traitor to his country and ancestors
And religion. McCormick got his wagon
Bogged the ground was that rotten it would bog
A duck in places. Another hawker named Ben Gould

Also were camped in Greta seen the wagon bogged
Gould had abandon his wagon for fear
Of losing his horses in the spewy ground
McCormicks horse galloped away. Mrs. McCormick

Accused me of working the horse Mr. and Mrs.
McCormick accused Gould of using the horse
Accused me of catching the horse for Gould
Said I was a liar. I who was not there at the time

I told him neither me or Ben Gould used their horse
Gould wrapped up a note and a pair of calves testicles
Gave the parcel to a boy told him to give them
To Mrs. McCormick. In that way he gave it to her husband

I followed him in the dust where the post and rail
Was taking down. Mrs. McCormick struck my horse
In the flank with a bullock's shin it jumped forward
My fist came in collision with Mr. McCormick's nose

McCormick said Gould and me used his horse
Mrs. McCormick gave good substantial evidence I pleaded
Gould's innocence for 12 months Consequently
I got 3 months for delivering the parcel

Threats and Revenge

You are committing a manifest injustice
In imprisoning so many innocent people
My character could not be painted blacker
Than it as present and is my brothers and sisters
And my mother not to be pitied?
I shall be forced to seek revenge
On a parcel of big ugly fat-necked wombat
Headed big bellied magpie legged

Narrow hipped splaw-footed sons
Of Irish Bailiffs or English landlords.
And why not make it public to avenge my cause?
Any Policeman or other man who do not
Throw up their arms directly as I call on them
Knows the consequence Which is a speedy
Dispatch to Kingdom Come. I do not wish to give
The order full force without giving timely warning

I will seek revenge for the name and character
Which has been given to me and my relations. I will
Be compelled to show some colonial stratagem
Something different to shooting three troopers in self defence
I would manure the Eleven Mile with their bloated carcasses
Their fat taken out rendered poured down their throat boiling
Beware for we are now desperate men. Do not attempt
To reside in Victoria. I am a widow's son Outlawed
And my orders must be obeyed

For A Smile From Julia

I take the liberty in addressing
A few remarks to you. I write these lines
Hoping. My chief reason for writing
This is to tell you I was riding the mare

Through Greta to find you returning home.
I thought it was the truth. I went to our camp
All of true blood bone and beauty
We thought it best to try enough to lie down

I make a statement take no offense
My conscience is as clear as the snow in Peru
I have arrived safe over the Murray
Soon after I left there was a warrant

For me so I left the colony and became
A rambling gambler night and day for three weeks
It was impossible for me to be in Victoria
As every schoolboy knows me

We thought we knew our doom was sealed
I have no more paper unless I rob for it
I don't think there is a man born
Could have the patience to suffer what I did

I would like to know you
People would say I was a decent gentleman
And as purely innocent as the child unborn
Or I would have quietly rode away

And so I came back to Victoria
I spent and will again spend many a happy day
Fearless free and bold what pleasure I will do
With a woman her breasts a wet spring

About the Author

Nathanael O'Reilly is an Irish-Australian poet; he teaches creative writing at the University of Texas at Arlington. His nine previous poetry collections include *Dear Nostalgia* (above/ground press, 2023), *Boulevard* (Beir Bua Press, 2021), *(Un)belonging* (Recent Work Press, 2020), *BLUE* (above/ground press, 2020), *Preparations for Departure* (UWAP, 2017) and *Distance* (Ginninderra Press, 2015). His poetry appears in over one hundred journals and anthologies published in fourteen countries, including *Anthropocene, Bealtaine Magazine, Cordite Poetry Review, The Elevation Review, Howl: New Irish Writing, New World Writing Quarterly, Mascara Literary Review, Skylight 47, Trasna* and *Westerly*. He is the poetry editor for *Antipodes: A Global Journal of Australian/New Zealand Literature*.

Praise for the Author

'Borrow[ing]' from Kelly's letters, 'Wombat[-]clever' O'Reilly has moulded found poetry that is 'Fearless free and bold' as the Australian bushranger. His lines 'gallop' like the 'Stallion[s] the greatest horsestealer borrow[ed].

Stuart Barnes. Poet. *Like to the Lark* (2023), *Glasshouses* (2016).

In *Selected Poems of Ned Kelly*, O'Reilly allows the famed outlaw's inventive sentences room to breathe and perform anew the rebelliousness which 'made the country ring / with the name of Kelly.'

Toby Davidson. Poet and author of *Good for the Soul: John Curtin's Life with Poetry.*